Renewal

Lived and learned
advice to give.

Anne McKeown
Emma Carter
Nancy Nouaimeh
Clare Reilly
Ana Caragea
Julie Casey
Olga Hogan
Sarah Morgan
Lisa Sweeney
Kistin Gunnis
Karen Tisdell

For further information and any questions visit our website at www.businessinheels.com
Email: info@businessinheels.com

ISBN: 978-0-6451639-3-3 (paperback)

Typeset by Karinya Kreations, www.kkreations.design

Edited by Steve Sweeney

Compiled, produced, and published by Business in Heels International Pty Ltd

Contents

Foreword

Advice comes and goes.

Some you cling to like your grandmother's scone recipe, other gems are discarded like old soup bones and other pieces of it seem like travesties of justice when you realise how valuable they were well after the use-by date of the problems they were designed to overcome.

Some advice is handed down through generations and never even recognised as advice until much later. Like the way you brush your teeth, tie your laces or set your table.

At the time of learning these, they may have seemed as though they would never be useful as these were tasks you didn't really enjoy performing. Then you create your own next generation to hand them down to and discordant music chimes in your ears as your own progeny question the value of this knowledge, just as you did 40 years earlier.

Some advice comes in the form of opinions which have never been tested yet the speaker

FOREWORD

feels confident to pass them on as wisdom. Spur of the moment thoughts which are vocalised since the speaker feels a need to contribute to a conversation and not look wanting or empty of thought.

Then there's the advice that strikes a chord deep within you because time and tide and geography and relationships and love and destiny all conspired to make the receiving of it a welcome or necessary experience.

Regardless of the form, one may use words of wisdom on one person and they are wasted while for another those same words can instil a potion so powerful as to transform a life. And, sometimes, it's the nature of one's relationship to the giver which dictates the manner in which it is received and interpreted.

It may provoke a cause to pause, a need for speed, a yearning for learning or a passion for dashin'.

Yet perhaps the most important aspect is not whether advice is right or wrong, good or bad, timely or late. Perhaps the most important aspect is that it came from the heart, because someone cared enough to share an experience and what they learned from it so you may ruminate and decide if it should apply to you.

Dear reader, please enjoy...
Renewal. Lessons learned and advice given.

"With laser sharp focus and a load of hard work,
I had it all by the time I was 28

...

And just when I thought life couldn't get better it all came crashing down."

Anne McKeown

Anne McKeown

Anne McKeown, the owner of 2Mpower Coaching is a highly regarded Master Coach. She champions women as individuals and business owners.

Through her Reignite Your Spark program she empowers women to step up, speak up and show up with confidence in all areas of life, so they can enjoy more success and happiness.

Anne incorporates various tools and techniques when coaching or facilitating individuals and teams because she says, "it's not enough to tell people what to do - it's essential to show them HOW to do it." She believes every woman has a unique gift to offer the world and sees it as her job to help them find it, use it and soar on the wings of it!

Anne is a published author. Her book Take Back Control of Your Life Now is a blueprint to learn from the past and create the future you want. She is also the founder of Sydney Women's Self-Empowerment Meetup which has over 700 members.

Anne is a wife and mother to two daughters Maris & Megan, (the 2Ms in 2Mpower) for whom she strives to be a positive role model.

Anne is able to assist you by offering her expertise as a coach, inspiring speaker and facilitator.

Website	annemckeown.com
LinkedIn	linkedin.com/in/anne-mckeown-2mpower
Facebook	facebook.com/2Mpower.co
Instagram	instagram.com/anne_mckeown_coach/
Twitter	twitter.com/2Mpower_

by Anne McKeown

Success is a feeling on the Inside

As the youngest in a family of 8, living in a 2-bedroom council flat in Glasgow, I often heard my mother complain, "There's not enough space and there's never enough money." At a young age I decided I would always have plenty of both.

For years, I followed all the guru advice. With laser sharp focus and a load of hard work, I had it all by the time I was 28: my own home, a rich corporate career, flash company car, European holidays and spare cash in the bank. Plus, I had Rob, my handsome and generous boyfriend.

And just when I thought life couldn't get better it all came crashing down.

My boss invited me to London to discuss changes in the company structure. The plan was to get rid of all licensees (because they took one third of all profit) and replace them with managers, who would be paid a basic annual salary.

by Anne McKeown

"But I can't do that!" I bemoaned to my boss. "I've worked with these people for 8 years helping them build their businesses and now you want me to make them redundant and remove their livelihood!"

"Well, if you don't, someone else will." He replied.

I couldn't wait to get home and discuss it all with Rob, he was my sounding board and always helped me see things from a different perspective. He was a naval officer and while I'd been in London his ship was docked in Europe. I called the ship, (this was in the days before mobile phones and social media – we hadn't talked for days).

"Rob, isn't here, he's been in a car crash and is in ICU at hospital," his friend Gavin told me.

"OMG! Where? I must see him."

"You can't."

"Why the hell not?"

"His wife is with him!"

Gavin spoke on about how miserable Rob was in his marriage and how he was planning to divorce his wife to be with me... I dropped the telephone receiver. I felt like an astronaut floating in space with nothing to ground me. "*How did I not see it? Was everything a lie? How could I have been so stupid? Did I imagine it all?*" I ran to the kitchen where I had a little box full of mementoes. Phew! It was all there – handwritten poetry, love letters, pressed flowers, photos of us together laughing. I fell to the floor and sobbed.

My family and friends suggested I was better off without him. They called Rob names I can't put into print.

Unable to cope, I visited the doctor. He gave me pills to dull the pain. For days, I hid under my duvet with Johnnie Walker, listening to Annie Lennox's song *Cold*, the chorus going around and around my tired mind... "Dying is easy. It's living that scares me to death!"

One morning, a thud on my wooden hall floor woke me up. I dragged myself out of bed to see what it was. The postman had dropped a heavy envelope through the letterbox. I opened it to find an invitation. Smiling back at me was a photo of Rob, in his white uniform, looking as dashing as ever. I turned it over and read *Order of Funeral Service*. The date was 4 days prior. No one had invited me to the funeral of my lover and best friend. Inside it read: The pastor asks that everyone pray for *Rob's wife and child*. My legs melted below me. I fell against the wall and howled. In that moment, I made the decision to quit my job, give back my company car, rent out my apartment and get as far away as I could from this grief, guilt and shame.

For 3 years, I volunteered across the globe with nothing but a backpack of essentials. The people who crossed my path slowly melted my hardened heart and mended my wounded spirit. I found true success laughing with a leper in India, washing the feet of a homeless woman in Australia and helping a blind man in Africa to see. I received priceless gifts: a hymn of appreciation sung by local villagers; a look that said, "Thank You" from the heart, a firm handshake that confirmed a lifetime connection; a hug that caused me to breakdown and break through to a new positive way of living life.

I have come to realise that success is not about the quantity of material possessions we have. Success is not an external badge of honour. It is a state that causes us to smile on the inside. Success is the feeling we are rewarded with when we do or make something that creates a positive change in others. It is the sense of satisfaction we experience from living a worthwhile life, a life that has a positive impact on those around us and ourselves. As human beings, when we do what we love, we experience joy. Add helping others to the mix and we are rewarded with an avalanche of positive feelings. This is real success.

I ought to thank Rob and my old boss because their betrayals led me to re-evaluate my life and realise that my day-to-day existence was out of whack. Back then, I had little free time, lots of stress, hardly any fun. I took everything too seriously and I constantly compared myself to everyone else who seemed to be doing better than me (and that was before the days of Instagram!)

These experiences led me to start my own coaching business with a passion to empower women who feel lost and are searching for purpose. Women who are capable but lack belief in themselves or their business. Women who procrastinate and don't achieve their goals. Women who put everyone else first and struggle to speak their truth. If that's you, then I invite you to give yourself permission to live the life you were born to live and make a promise to not give up until you achieve it! Take ownership of your present situation, reach out and ask for help and acknowledge that continued success requires continued growth.

“In desperation one day, I walked out the front door of my home with nothing but my son. Fear was my driver, self-preservation my compass.”

Emma Carter

Emma Carter

In many ways, my role as Customer Relations Manager with Business in Heels is like being the concierge at a maxed-up glam resort and convention centre for women.

When they first arrive, many are a little lost; unsure of what to do, who to speak to, where to go and, for some, why they are even there! So I become very inquisitive and listen and ask and listen and ask some more. With knowledge of their desires, needs, concerns and expectations, it's then possible for me to guide, advise, assist and direct them to options, people and resources within the organisation that will connect them with the improved outcomes they seek.

It's wonderful to be regularly able to make this positive difference in their lives. In turn, the knowledge and wisdom coming to me from them further helps me help others. Give, receive and give some more... I love this part!

And who doesn't love a side-hustle? When people in our semi-rural neighbourhood go on holiday, they call me to care for their menageries and make sure everything is safe and secure until they return.

In my spare time, mountain biking, walking Princess and performing benchtop experiments with my son happily take up the rest of my days.

LinkedIn | linkedin.com/in/emma-carter-b79a95a0

by Emma Carter

Taking my own advice.

Sitting at McDonald's with my son in his pram at 11pm, rain poured down like the tears I had been shedding. Fearing going home, but not sure where else to go, I promised him life would get better than this. It had to.

The person I thought I knew was now no more than a myth and I realised my life read like a horror novel. I had become trapped in it, consumed by it and now every piece of who I was had been stripped from me. I sat watching the rain, suffocating in self-doubt.

In desperation one day, I walked out the front door of my home with nothing but my son. Fear was my driver, self-preservation my compass. I was incredibly blessed that a dear friend was able to come to my aid. In hindsight, I wish I'd taken my passport and licence as filling out forms and proving my identity without them became a real issue. And suddenly... there was a lot of paperwork to fill out! Sadly, trying to retrieve them or anything else was impossible despite the advice from the police who suggested my female friend and I go over and try and to get them ourselves and they would attend if something happened. Absolutely not worth the risk. Thinking back, I am horrified any women in my position would be told this.

Eventually, my son and I returned to my family home. I felt overwhelmed and was trapped in a foreboding sense of failure. I was now a single mum with no money, no job and living back home with mum.

During those first 12 months, I began a mental rebuild to let go of anger, what should have been and, somehow, tried to determine a new future. I focused on my son and tried to give him as many positive experiences as possible. Seeing him develop from a baby into an energetic toddler with a very outgoing personality was a form of therapy itself.

When I thought of stepping back into the workforce, I was at a loss. I didn't want to and couldn't go back to my previous career as a chemist. With my confidence only a shadow of what it once was, I now doubted my ability to fulfil any number of roles. You see, there was the voice, the one stuck in my head telling me I wouldn't be any good at that, not qualified enough or not experienced enough. Some days, it was all I could hear.

I was lucky that a friend of mine saw something in me which I did not. She was resigning from her position and felt that I would be a better fit for the role. So here began my journey with Business in Heels. I was sitting across from

Lisa with a cup of earl grey tea and being asked if I could handle a database, (not so difficult, the voice said) and call customers (I said yes, but to be honest, for that first 6 months, every time before I picked up the phone it gave me a fair amount of anxiety!) Slowly, the voice returned and allowed the self-doubt to creep back too because, well... why would anyone want to talk to me?

Yet little by little, phone call by phone call, I started to actually enjoy these conversations. Hearing about people's stories, passions and learning all about their business or career goals fascinated me. A very special part of my job is getting to follow the journeys of our customers over their time with us. I am the first point of contact for many who come across Business in Heels and the person they call when things don't quite go as planned. I have taken great pride in being able to guide and direct them.

The first lockdown of the pandemic in 2020 saw me no longer just telling people about our services and upcoming events but helping to guide so many of our business owners towards as many supports as possible. Encouraging them to attend a coffee connection to prevent them becoming isolated, a mentor morning to get them some advice and sometimes just an ear to listen. I still remember walking one business owner through the Centrelink process after she had closed her business.

It was a revelation to me... my knowledge was able to help others! What I had learned through study and from a vast collection of acquired knowledge of so many diverse businesses had given me an incredible perspective. I have a valuable contribution to make. Me!

In person networking with a room full of complete strangers is either something we thrive on or just the thought of it leaves us wanting to hide away. Many of the women I meet are from the latter group, of which I have spent quite a lot of time as a member too. It's amazing how many of us have our own destructive voices telling us we are not worthy.

Three years ago, I would have been incapable of this...

I was offered the opportunity to represent Business in Heels at Top 50 Awards Night as Lisa and our PR manager had prior commitments. I found myself facing a room of over 100 incredible small business owners and not one of them had I ever encountered before! That first conversation was definitely the hardest. However, once the ice was broken, I realised we all had something in common, a heart-felt passion for what we do. I made some wonderful connections that night. We must never let our fear and negative self-talk keep us from incredible opportunities. I found that, in a way, I had to accept the fear and still push my way through by putting one foot in front of the other. Doing so enabled me to walk up to that first person and say hi. That first one is always the hardest!

In life, it's important to be open to opportunity and possibility and not let those voices hold us back. Take what is presented with both hands. I am always encouraging others to overcome the black cloud of self-doubt and I doubt we are ever completely free of it. Yet that other voice, the one coming from deep in your soul, listen to it. You see, every time you step outside your comfort zone you are feeding it, making it stronger than the anxiety telling you you can't do it.

I was honoured to be asked to write a chapter in this book... and a little terrified. (Cue that chorus of little voices!) So here I am taking my own advice and not letting them win. I want to encourage you to do the same. You are good enough, you can achieve your goals, your contribution is important, your story has meaning, and I hope one day you will share it with me.

That fearful night in McDonald's now seems like such a long time ago. That terrified single mum who sat there watching the rain now has purpose, a few goals of her own and loves to play with her son in those colourful, S-bending climbing tubes.

"...I would have been perceived as a dominant, tough and unemphatic colleague and manager."

Nancy Nouaimeh

Nancy Nouaimeh

Nancy is an energetic business leader, mentor, and culture transformation expert with an extensive expertise in Scientific and System thinking, Organizational Excellence, Quality Management, and Integrated Management Systems.

She has a passion for the implementation of Excellence Models and Principles. Her work with organizations facilitates a robust continuous improvement process and outstanding achievements.

Holder of two Masters' degrees in Total Quality Management, and in Agronomic Sciences & Bioengineering from Belgium, Nancy has published several book chapters and articles related to Risk Management, Quality and Excellence. She is a Chartered Business Excellence Expert (BEX-Ireland),

Certified Organizational Excellence Specialist (OES -Canada) and is a long-term member leader of the American Society for Quality (ASQ). In addition, she has expertise in National, International and Government Excellence Awards. In 2022, Nancy was Awarded the Global Women in Leadership Award from GCPIT.

She is the founder of Xcellium Management Consultancy, the first licensed affiliate of the Shingo Institute (USA) in the Middle East and Africa. But what she is most proud of as a mom, is her two amazing adolescent triathletes, a living example that "Excellence is a Habit".

Website	xcelliumconsulting.com
LinkedIn	linkedin.com/in/nancy-nouaimeh-215a467
Facebook	facebook.com/Nancy.Nouaimeh
Instagram	instagram.com/nancynouaimeh
Twitter	twitter.com/NNouaimeh

by Nancy Nouaimeh

A Rookie's rocky start

My sister and I are both Virgos. Virgos are excellent friends and partners. We are methodical, quick thinkers, perfectionists and can be meticulous in our pursuit of improvement.

So, can you imagine how it would be to work with a Virgo, rookie, hands-on Quality Control Manager with a passion for excellence and no experience to back it up? Well 17 years ago, people had to in my first job working in the United Arab Emirates.

I was in a new country with a new culture and I was ready for a new adventure. Full of aspirations and enthusiasm, I was assigned to establish a quality management department from scratch, build a team and work with colleagues on setting standards and projects for continuous improvement. Having studied Total Quality Management concepts, majoring in tools and methods, I felt well-equipped to succeed in this mission and create the impact

I desired in my new organisation. This energy booster, which was added to my Virgo/rookie blend, enthused me and crafted a unique get-up-and-do attitude which I was so proud of. Ideas and plans about how to improve existing systems and projects flowed easily in me.

The next step was to execute them.

As you know, it always takes two to tango, so no plan is ever a one-woman show. So slowly, the challenge of executing the plans with and through people and leading projects in a multicultural environment started to unfold. The fire that was in me, the belief that things can be done right the first time (as I was taught at the university) and the rush to achieve and succeed became my self-inflicted challenges. As I started working with colleagues, I realise now I did not give the necessary time to know them, their potential, their stories, their history and mostly their own challenges and whether my expectations were understood and realistic in setting up project deadlines. You won't be surprised to learn such things were not part of my university degree.

And no surprise either that my colleagues' tolerance for my comments on their shortfalls, lack of results and their opinions of me diminished with time. After all, I would have been perceived as a dominant, tough and unemphatic colleague and manager.

Naturally, my boss, the CEO at that time, started hearing stories (in my defence, many were overly spiced-up) about how hard I am on people, how irritating I could become when there were no or incorrect results. These stories turned the person who was my first fan into someone who felt the need to constantly bring this issue to my attention. Sometimes this came in a humorous way like joking with my kids whenever they came to visit me in the office and asking, "What is mummy like at home? Is she tough on you too?" or, "How can you keep up with her?"

At first, this was heartbreaking. It took a lot of reflection and analysis to find the equilibrium that could make both my CEO and I satisfied and convinced of a way to move forward which took advantage of my skills in a constructive way. Yet so many questions kept coming back to me: Who is right? What do I need to do more of? Or less? Is there a real need to change? And what to change? How to adjust and still achieve? How to bring others on board?

I lived these dilemmas for months. It impacted my health, my morale and my relationship with my colleagues to the extent that I was thinking of quitting my job.

But quitting for a Virgo is not an option. There's a fine line between determined and stubborn and we Virgos sometimes struggle to see the difference.

Instead of quitting, I re-evaluated the situation. I had several discussions with colleagues and read some interesting books about leadership and high-performing teams. My epiphany was to focus on the positive elements of this experience and put the brakes on the accumulating guilt and self-doubt.

It is very easy to self-destruct when we lose our compasses. As a rookie confronted with criticism, it was hard to see clearly at first and negative emotions clouded my judgement. The most valuable advice my CEO gave me was contained in a note on my office door, "Shit happens but life goes on". So, I took a step backward, learned to ask the right questions and listened to what others had to say. Understanding my own culture, the culture of the organisation and what was most important for us to succeed as a team became paramount. And yes, I started taking myself less seriously. It was not about achieving less. It was about achieving more with a different approach. I became more inclusive and empathic, had more conversations, smiled more and began to enjoy my work.

Neither my CEO nor I were completely right or wrong. We simply had different views and approaches to work. It was only when things became very difficult to handle that each of us took time to understand the other's perspective. As a result, the wider group of colleagues followed the lead and adjusted. So much so that numerous strong relationships and teams were built and produced amazing outcomes for the organisation.

The main lesson learned from this experience was always use the Plan-Do-Check-Act methodology... even in relationships. And whatever your drivers and motivations are, if they do not fit in the ecosystem you are working in, you need to find the middle-ground.

Stay true to yourself, be authentic *and* reconsider your approach when needed. Trust and respect are earned and relationships and teams are built. Iterations are needed. I wish

I'd understood this earlier. Moreover, a growth mindset is a recipe for success, never stop learning and improving. Embrace your failures. They often contain the best lessons.

My work with companies on culture transformation, building high-performing teams and achieving excellence by design is built on my conviction that "Leading with Humility" and "Respecting every Individual" are key cultural enablers. They are fundamental traits of exceptional leaders who bring the best out of people and help them fulfill their potential.

And yes, Virgos can do this well once they realise the value of nurturing human capital.

“So, with each painful step around the beautiful, secluded, off-grid property, and my shameful secret bubbling under the surface, my ability, mobility and mental health declined.”

Clare Reilly

Clare Reilly

Clare Reilly (she/her) was diagnosed with multiple sclerosis (MS) in April 2017. With a background in outdoor education, Clare loves to spend time outdoors, albeit slightly differently these days.

Clare lives on the Bellarine Peninsula, near Geelong, with her husband and son, and loves an early morning dip in Port Phillip Bay. Clare is a creative, who loves to try her hand at various arts and crafts, including painting, ceramics, booknooks (seriously, check them out) and is passionate about sharing really good food with loved ones.

Clare is an advocate for those living with MS and other chronic illnesses. She shares funny, sometimes confronting and thought-provoking posts and Reels on Instagram. Clare hosts the podcast MS Understood - conversations about multiple sclerosis with people from all over the world. She loves the community feel and support she both gives and receives via Instagram and through the podcast. A question Clare asks at the end of every podcast episode is "what is the best thing to have happened because you were diagnosed with MS?" Clare's answer is the incredible community that she has discovered, the empathy she has developed and the self-awareness and confidence that has emerged since diagnosis.

Website	clarereilly.com
LinkedIn	linkedin.com/in/clare-reilly-85a3301ba
Facebook	facebook.com/ClareReillyadvocate
Instagram	instagram.com/clare.reilly

by Clare Reilly

Choosing Control

We arrived at the front gate. It was the first step to entering our new home and beginning our new job of running the outdoor education centre. I took in the surroundings. From the base of the Victorian Alpine National Park, mountains rose around us and drew us into the valley we were to call home. The blue sky and crisp, still air heralded a clear winter's day.

Transferring our belongings from our car into a work vehicle and buckling in our two-and-a-half-year-old son was the first step of many. Once secured, we drove 2km through the privately owned front paddock along an unmaintained farm track which followed the Macalister River to our parking area. Then we moved our belongings to human-powered rickshaws and pulled them 200m to the access of the outdoor education camp we were now employed to manage. We parked the rickshaws and proceeded to walk up and down a small rocky hill with our arms laden to load up the flying fox that would send all our worldly possessions 100m across and 50m above the river. Through this whole exhausting journey, the anticipation of managing staff, students and the property weighed on me with a sense of excited trepidation.

And all the while a loud voice was screaming at me, reminding me of the multiple sclerosis diagnosis I had received two weeks earlier.

I had not told my employers or the community of the camp that the reason I used hiking poles to get around the 20-acre property was multiple sclerosis, it meant each of my steps carried an ever-increasing sense of shame. It also meant I felt the need to prove myself, to myself, to my employers, to my family. We all needed to see I could still work my dream job despite the condition I hadn't come to terms with and they didn't know I had. So, with each painful step around the beautiful, secluded, off-grid property, and my shameful secret bubbling under the surface, my ability, mobility and mental health declined.

The days were long, sometimes 16 hours, and the responsibility was next level. We were managing and living with our team of six twenty-something-year-old staff, being on-call while groups of students were out hiking and parenting and home-schooling our son. Additionally, we were responsible for all administration of running an outdoor education centre while having no internet or electricity. It was exhausting. Add living with a chronic illness on top of all that and I simply couldn't fight the fatigue. One day, I lay on the rug in front of the fire naked after a shower my husband had to help me in and out of. I was unable to get up. I felt helpless. All dignity had faded out of me and dissolved into the rug as I sobbed. The tears only highlighted the overwhelming sense of loss I felt. Loss of autonomy, loss of self, loss of control over my body. I was at rock bottom and couldn't see a way back up.

I numbed myself. To the outside I was living this outrageous, cool, off-the-grid life but I was using this to numb and hide from my diagnosis. I was the ostrich with its head in the sand. I filled my days with administration, gardening, staff training and home-schooling my son. I made myself so busy that I didn't have a chance to process, even acknowledge, my diagnosis. In the rare moments of stillness I found, anger and denial consumed me. Usually having a positive demeanour, I succumbed to being dark and temperamental. I blamed work, though deep down I knew it was because of a part of myself I hadn't come to terms with yet. This lack of control over my emotions plagued me in my darkest hours.

Once our contract of managing the facility had finished and we returned to our home and community by the coast, I started allowing myself to process the diagnosis I'd been given two-and-a-half-years earlier. When my energy didn't return after a few weeks of resting, the realisation hit me... this was real, and it wasn't going away. I was deep in grief, despair and shame. I was so angry. I metaphorically threw my hands up in the air and relinquished more autonomy and control to the medical system. Feeling overwhelmed by everything I hadn't dealt with for the last 2 years, I started seeing professionals who could help manage my declining symptoms.

Initially, I said yes to everyone. Welcoming half-rate therapists into my medical and support team. I felt so helpless and was grateful to anyone who was willing to spin a tale that'd have me envisaging a multiple sclerosis-less me. I wanted to be cured and was willing to employ anyone who could promise that.

A physiotherapist I saw for a year was more interested in telling me their life problems and finding a friend than working with me toward my vision of maintaining my mobility. I only felt confident to fire them after 12 months. And was a lot more cautious and considered when hiring the next.

Hiring, I say. Yes, our support team of health care professionals are employed by us. We are the boss, surrounded by professionals in their field, and the 'project', the job, the goal is to support us to be the best we can be. Should anyone not fulfill their role, then they will be let go. Fired from their position, with a more appropriate employee to fill their job description.

Taking control is the best piece of advice that I wish I had taken earlier.

The feelings of self-assuredness, confidence and autonomy returned back to my consciousness. I may have an uncontrollable, debilitating disease, but I could be in control of how I was looked after, cared for and treated by the medical professionals that I choose to engage with.

"I wish I didn't blame myself for crying, for feeling deeply, for feeling too much all at once. I was tough on myself. I thought I had to figure out life fast and by myself."

Ana Caragea

Ana Caragea

Ana Caragea is an Award-Winning Leadership Coach, the first GC Index® Partner in the UAE, the first IAPPC Certified Positive Psychology Coach®, and the Founder of Strategic Discovery, a leadership coaching and mentoring company for introvert managers and leaders, helping them lead with courage and self-awareness.

Ana has been coaching since 2014, having a University degree in Psychology and Sociology, a GC Index® accreditation, and a Hogan Personality Assessments certification. Her clients range from Managing Directors, CEOs and CFOs to Sales Executives and HR Managers.

On a personal note, she is an introvert, an avid book reader and an F1 fan. She's married and enjoys watching the Formula 1 races with her husband.

Some of the Workshops & Webinars Ana did are: *The 5 crucial mistakes to avoid when leading remote teams, How introverts can leverage their strengths when working in diverse teams, Can women balance it all, From Manager to Leader - 7 Must-Have Skills of Resilient Leaders, How to become a Game Changer as an Entrepreneur, The ABC of Inner Peace/ Mental Resilience, Leading with Courage, Happiness at Work, How Procrastination is impacting Time Management, Customer Service Excellence,* and *Safety Awareness Training* - based on Hogan Personality Inventory.

Website | anacaragea.com
LinkedIn | linkedin.com/in/anacaragea
Facebook | facebook.com/coachAnaCaragea
Instagram | instagram.com/ana_caragea
Twitter | twitter.com/AnaCaragea

by Ana Caragea

The journey **within.**

Dear reader,
the emotional storm you have within you is normal. If you feel intense inner pressure, know that you might be going through a human experience of emotional pain.

Know that after the storm has died down, the sun will rise again, the shore will clear, and you'll have gained insight into how resourceful and strong you are.

Your tears are not a sign of weakness.

No, they signify a release of energy that has built up within you while searching for a way out. Your inner beauty is shining and warming the outside world.

This is what I wish I had known when I was growing up and a teenager. I wish I didn't blame myself for crying, for feeling deeply, for feeling too much all at once. I was tough on myself. I thought I had to figure out life fast and by myself. I was not alone, I had resources around me (my parents, grandparents, friends), but I didn't know I could share that part of me.

You see, in my family, we didn't talk about emotions. Well, at least not about these "other" emotions that some wouldn't call "positive". So, I learnt to keep it all to myself. My tears, pain, angst, sadness, and fear. Crying in the dark or when alone was something I did on a few occasions while growing up. As a kid feeling too much, I was unaware of what to do with all those feelings. There was no guiding manual for how to process and integrate my emotions and feelings. So I started pushing them to the side. I built walls around my heart, suffocating the emotions until I was numb.

What I wish I knew back then was that without the emotions that caused me to feel the emotional pain, I couldn't feel love either. Or at least, not at the intensity it deserved. When I blocked my tears, sadness, fear, anxiety, anger, and guilt, I also blocked my joy, love, and enthusiasm for life.

Love is meant to be felt with your heart open, with all of your being. I like to call it, "having your heart full of warmth, joy, and expansion". Yet I was merely aware of love as a concept. Sure, I cared for the people in my life, but there was no intensity and fullness in experiencing love. It was just a word I said or thought when I knew it was the right thing to say or think. Looking back, I can see the difference as now I understand how it is to love fully, to have your heart filled completely with love, to allow its magnitude.

Even my laughter is now different (my husband has shared this observation). When I laugh, I give myself permission to be fully present, to experience that moment with all of my being. The sound of joy is deeper, and it runs through my body. Before, I had a contained smile or laughter, as if not to upset anyone with it.

Now, as an introvert leader, I've recognised that I get to be the leader I wish I had seen while growing up. I've come to realise that if I wanted to see more compassion, kindness, and empathy in the world, I needed to allow myself to deeply sense these emotions and feelings beyond the superficial. Integrating my feelings allows me to see and help others going through a similar experience.

One of my mentors, Allison Crow, once said: "Your heart can hold it all." And I agree. The moment I stopped fighting and blaming my emotions for suffocating me, for making me feel so much, I came to see them as temporary. Once I'd let them run their course, they didn't hold onto me. Ebb and flow. There is a peak, a high intensity in my feelings and emotions, then there is the natural progression that lightens up my heart. And I breathe again and come back to my centre, where wisdom and inner alignment are present.

My emotions are now my guiding light. They are a signal, a compass to something deep within, an expression of life. And, back then, I didn't know that. I only knew it hurt too much, experiencing angst within my heart I didn't have an answer to. The truth I now know is that my heart desired expression, visibility, communication, fairness, understanding and purpose. Even at that earlier stage, I needed answers, I wanted a direction to help me focus my energy and an explanation for what I was experiencing.

Dear reader,

my wish for you after reading these rows is to learn how to be kind to yourself and to give your inner critic a break. Your emotions will indicate to you that you are alive and have a human experience. The how-to is different for each of you. Breathe, allow, let go. Find someone who can listen to you without judgement, without jumping in trying to cut short your experience of feeling your emotions. You are resourceful, and your wisdom will guide you if you allow it.

If you are at a point in life where you've lost hope or are feeling lost, without a purpose, know that your life matters.

How you feel matters.

Your experience is valid.

Reach out, and let's talk.

I've been there and what saved me was asking for help with my last energy resources. I was then able to process my emotions and feelings, to release the bottled-up energy through lots of crying and intense feeling. It helped me clear my mind, to settle and re-energise. I've regained my enthusiasm for living and excitement for creating a world I'd love to see.

What I wish I knew back then was that feeling deeply is a sign of strength, it's a testament of connection with life and with others. If you are feeling too much, too deeply, know that you are a gift to a numb and disconnected world. You are important and loved. Stay true to yourself and live fully with enthusiasm and joy!

Your supporter,
Ana.

“I struggled with self-harm and thoughts of suicide. Life didn’t seem worth living as I had little hope for the future.”

Julie Casey

Julie Casey

Julie is the founder and therapist at Nourishing Hearts Wellness Care Farm where she combines the care of the land and animals with the care of people.

Her educational background includes a Developmental Service Worker Diploma and both Bachelor and Master of Social Work degrees. She is also a certified Animal Assisted Therapist and certified Play Therapist.

She has enjoyed over 20 years working and volunteering in a variety of care settings, supporting individuals and families with different abilities across the lifespan who experience mental health, addiction, and disability challenges.

Julie has been in private practice since 2016 where she provides in-office talk therapy in addition to animal, nature, and play-based therapies for children, youth, adults, and families experiencing trauma, grief, loss, depression, anxiety, low self-esteem, autism, ADHD, FASD and for those struggling with self-harm & suicide.

Julie is also a care provider for local Indigenous communities and as a fly-in therapist for a northern First Nation community. The therapeutic relationship is at the heart of Julie's approach to help support, treat, and prevent mental health challenges.

Julie believes in "walking the talk" and is passionate about her own personal self-reflections, inner growth and healing journey from her head to her heart.

Facebook | facebook.com/JulieCaseyMSW.RSW
Instagram | instagram.com/inourishingheartsaai

by Julie Casey

a Journey from my Head to my Heart

I grew up on a farm, playing in magical gullies and making homes and forts in the corn fields of Elgin County in Ontario, Canada. I am the youngest of four girls.

As the youngest, I often found myself playing alone or making friends with any little creatures that I could find. I loved animals and nature. I struggled socially to fit in and was often the tag-along friend. I felt lost and did not know where I belonged. The world did not feel like a safe place to me. In my early teens, I was diagnosed with major depression and, with hindsight, I can see I was riddled with anxiety. I struggled with self-harm and thoughts of suicide. Life didn't seem worth living as I had little hope for the future. I dropped out of school and left home early which led to homelessness where I either lived out of a broken-down car or was outstaying my welcome on people's couches.

Life was lonely and painful.

by Julie Casey

I got married at the age of 20 and had two amazing children. Although having a family gave me a sense of purpose, I did not yet know who I was and I was constantly trying to be what I thought others wanted me to be. I could never measure up to expectations. I continued to struggle with self-degradation, anxiety and depression. I hid out from the world and isolated myself within my little family. The world was still an unsafe place for me.

Then... I got my first goats.

Sheep and chickens followed and I rejoiced as I discovered the comfort of my barn. No matter what was happening in my life and in my mind, I always felt better in the barn, sitting with my animals, telling them about my experiences and sharing my tears with them. I felt an affinity to animals that brought me deep comfort and my first sense of identity and belonging.

And somewhere deep inside, a crack of light opened as I realized my lived experiences could help others.

At 29, without a high school diploma, I mustered the courage to return to school in pursuit of becoming a social worker. It was a long journey of 13 years, but one that built confidence and belief within myself. Along this journey, I found myself learning, for the first time, about the Indigenous Peoples of Canada and the atrocities of colonialism. In no way am I comparing my pain and suffering to what Indigenous Peoples experienced, but in a small way I could relate to the pain that comes from a lack of belonging and the pain caused by uncertain identity. Even more so, I could relate to their deep connection to nature and animals and for the first time in my life I felt a sense of worth and validation for these connections and understanding of myself.

My exploration to understand the true history of the Indigenous Peoples of Canada led me to cross paths with Elders and Healers who were so kind to me and shared these three important lessons which I wish I knew earlier. They are lessons I carry with me each and every day and are now a part of my way of being in this world. First, the longest journey is from our head to our heart. I have come to understand it takes time to reconnect with our heart and to trust our heart to guide us in life, so we need to be gentle on ourselves as we learn. Unlearning old ways is possible but takes time. Second, know your truth. We all have truths and no matter what other people say or do, they can never take away our truths. We don't need other people's approval or validation for our experiences to be real. They are real to us. Lastly, I must stand in the face of fear and speak my truth. These teachings gave me the courage to honour who I am as a person and to embrace myself with love... just as I am.

In my case, fully honoring my authentic self meant stepping outside the traditional box of counseling by inviting animals and nature into my social work practice.

In 2014, I followed my heart and got two baby goats and my heart sang! I started a part-time mobile animal-assisted therapy service providing therapy to long-term care facilities. Shortly after I added sheep, chickens and a rabbit to my services and expanded to extend services to high schools, colleges and universities. I loved the work I was doing but it was fraught with others' skepticism and judgment since I was not working with the traditional therapy dog. Farm animals had not yet been recognized or valued as therapy animals. There were times when my methods were literally laughed at and dismissed as a valid therapeutic approach. During these times, I would remember the teachings and listen to my heart and trust my truths. It did not matter what other people thought, I knew the positive impact I was having upon my clients.

In 2017, my husband and I were fortunate to have the opportunity to purchase a 5-acre farm and Nourishing Hearts Wellness Care Farm was born. The farm means I can offer child, youth and adult counseling that includes traditional in-office talk therapy along with animal & nature assisted counselling and play therapy. I utilize a client-centered approach that encourages people to lead me where they feel comfortable talking. This may be sitting in the snuggle stall within the barn while cuddling and grooming animals or with a support animal with them in the office counselling space. Others feel more comfortable talking while doing arts & crafts, exploring the wetland, walking the meadow trail or sitting around a campfire. The empowerment that comes from this humanistic approach cultivates the trust and safety necessary for the journey to discover self, to experience what it is like to fit in and to feel a sense of belonging.

Now in 2022, in my 49th year, I walk my meadow trail and reflect upon my journey that has allowed for a heart-guided life that feels safe and abundant in gratitude. I am so thankful for my struggles as they have made me who I am today. I am grateful to have the opportunity to sit with others as they too experience the profound comfort of the barn and the nonjudgement and acceptance of animals.

I am so appreciative of the lessons shared with me that have allowed me to embrace my journey from my head to my heart, to know my truths and to face my fears so that I may be authentic to who I am. Most of all, I am thankful I can honour the little girl, who's heart was broken until she found the courage to connect whole-heartedly to animals and nature.

"Nonetheless, I was able to overcome those doubts by focusing on things that gave me energy. And all was right with the world until one day...

...somebody left a comment under one of my posts."

Olga Hogan, PhD

Olga Hogan

Originally from Estonia, Olga has lived, studied, and worked in Finland, England, Kazakhstan and now Australia.

While completing her PhD in Chemistry at Oxford, Olga was exposed to the vibrant startup community surrounding the university and shifted her focus to a combination of finance and innovation.

She joined Deloitte and qualified as a chartered accountant (now fellow), gaining direct experience across many businesses and investment areas.

During her corporate finance career Olga has worked in investor relations, private equity, and university research commercialisation. She also co-founded a predictive weather analytics start-up for energy traders in Europe.

Olga currently works with entrepreneurial researchers and innovative companies as a director at a large investment company, where she focuses her attention on university research commercialisation.

Olga is also an adjunct associate professor at Deakin University where she works on guided self-determination and its applications within the higher education and healthcare sectors.

Finally, she is busy building her second start-up – Franca – an online platform that enables teams to have better conversations and increase their emotional and social intelligence.

Website franca.coach

LinkedIn linkedin.com/in/olgahogan

Medium medium.com/@olgahogan

Offer If you would like to do a quick but insightful activity to find your superpowers, you can do so by visiting franca.coach/superpowers by Olga Hogan

Fire in the Belly

There is no "right" type of entrepreneur. The only common determinator is having "fire in the belly" about their start-up and idea.

When I co-founded my first technology start-up in Australia in 2009, there was not much information around what makes a "good" entrepreneur.

While doing my PhD in chemistry in the UK, I saw various university spinouts backed by venture capitalists (VCs). The founders, often senior academics, tended to take Chief Science Officer roles and bring in experienced CEOs to run the start-up. Later in my career working with start-ups at Deloitte, I again saw a similar pattern.

While continuing to work on the finance side of innovation, I read many interviews with various VC partners. Some insights were great, while others like, "entrepreneurs come up with innovative ideas" were counterproductive.

by Olga Hogan

My first start-up was a SaaS platform providing real-time weather and energy generation data to energy traders. The idea belonged to my co-founder, who was a software engineer and data scientist. He focused on all things regarding data analytics and software, leaving all non-technology aspects to me. And there were plenty: competitors' analysis, developing pricing, licensing agreements, IP protection, insurance and setting up partnerships to name a few.

I had fun doing all the strategy and finance. Yes, some things were draining (cold calling potential clients, dealing with tax offices in various countries) but it felt good to overcome those challenges. I had so much energy that I even started a blog in which I wrote about the finance and compliance issues I was learning about as part of our start-up.

Yet, in the background, I had a constant niggling feeling that I was not a real entrepreneur nor co-founder. Something just didn't seem right about applying that label to myself. Nonetheless, I was able to overcome those doubts by focusing on things that gave me energy. And all was right with the world until one day...

...somebody left a comment under one of my posts.

An anonymous commentator implied that since the idea was not mine... I was not a real entrepreneur.

The moment you see your hidden fears spelled out on the screen for the world to see is gut-wrenching. I felt nauseous. It was official, I was just an imposter who plays in start-ups and now

I knew that everyone knew!

I thought, "What the hell am I doing? I have recently moved to Australia and have no friends here because most of the time I am working on something which I have no claim to!" My energy levels declined. I even struggled to keep my motivation for doing tasks I was good at. I took down my blog. (In hindsight, I should have never opened it up for comments.)

Not thinking clearly, and desperate to find ways to contribute to the business idea, I convinced my co-founder that I could help with making the platform look nice from a design and user experience perspective. This desperation to prove and validate myself led to not fully looping in others and me hiring the wrong agency which resulted in production and release delays.

I hit rock bottom. I was also pregnant at this stage and had very limited options to deal with my emotions. So, I stayed in bed and Googled all I could about "the right type of entrepreneur".

A few very unproductive days later, I accidently saw an article where an entrepreneur, Anthony Tjan, mentioned that when he evaluates early-stage entrepreneurs, he looks for that "fire in the belly" and a "dare to be great" attitude.

That article changed everything for me because...

"Damn it! When I started, I had that fire in my belly and I was daring to be great. Daring enough to focus 100% of my time on it. So how did I let this feeling disappear and what can I do to get it back?"

Being a scientist, I decided to go back to what worked. By focusing on budgets, cash flow and strategy, the things that energised me, I was able to get that fire back. It felt great doing things I was good at.

I was brave enough to have a conversation with my co-founder about what was going on in my head. Having that frank conversation made us discuss and evaluate how we allocated roles within the company. Yes, there were tasks neither of us liked doing. But the realisation that the tasks I was good at were often the tasks that my co-founder had no interest in doing, was transformational.

This six months of unravelling and reforming gave me permission to bring the "whole me" to our start-up. I realised I did not have to own the idea. I just needed to recognise it as a great idea and be fired up about it. Which I did.

When the time came to plan our next five years, we realised that perhaps we should exit the start-up by selling the technology, an insight I may not have had if not for my previous finance experience.

Later in my career, I worked for an investment firm and was responsible for assessing the companies of other entrepreneurs. I saw for myself that all founders and co-founders are really quite different. The only constant was that "fire in the belly" and a strong self-awareness of why they do what they do.

Now when I work with start-ups, I still hear many founders questioning themselves or see non-technical co-founders trying to take on too much work in an ill-informed attempt to "prove their worth". This drains them as much it drained me and leads to founder burnout.

When I see this, I encourage entrepreneurs to look inside and find their invisible superpowers, those activities and tasks that energise them and keep the fire in their belly burning.

"I had brain fog, it felt like I was coasting, weighed down, overwhelmed and this was causing lacklustre productivity."

Sarah Morgan

Sarah Morgan

Sarah is a Speaker, MC, Panel Facilitator, Boardroom Facilitator and Leadership Expert, with a vision to change the way organisations think and behave, Sarah works with leaders in a multitude of industries to be able to empower their team, culture and create a world of thoughtful leaders.

Sarah developed the Influential Leaders Academy through studying human behaviour in the workplace, through years of coaching 100's of business owners and executives as they circumnavigated their career.

Recognising that meticulous behaviour adjustments and communication techniques enabled executives to move through their careers faster by gaining a better understanding of why they are where they are and how to move forward with a powerful plan and direction.

Discovering these techniques herself as she navigated her own leadership journey. Starting in large global corporations through to trail blazing for small businesses she recognised the mind set changes required to be a leader.

We can read about the very first step of the magnitude of events that happen for a leadership transformation to begin in Sarah's personal internal journey of self-development.

Website	sarahmorgan.com.au
LinkedIn	linkedin.com/in/sarah-morgan-business-coach
Facebook 1	facebook.com/GrowBusinessandWealth
Facebook Group	facebook.com/groups/leadershipinbusiness
Facebook 2	facebook.com/ChatwithSarahMorgan
Instagram	instagram.com/sarahmorganc2g
Offer	*The Influential Leader Academy and Network* is designed as a hands on coaching program for ambitious people wanting the skills to excel in business and life. Available for dynamic individuals and organisations wanting to enhance leadership effectiveness. See more details here: www.linktr.ee/influentialleader

by Sarah Morgan

The road to Liberation by building self worth.

Turning around hard times to become strong and resilient.

We all wish we could go back in time and give our younger selves some sage advice. Well, I'm no different.

Maybe it would have helped me avoid some of the heartache I've experienced, or maybe it would have given me a head-start in accomplishing my goals. Here are the things I would tell myself if I could go back to my younger self. Take these words to heart, they'll help you on your road to becoming a strong woman.

Don't be too concerned about how others see you, even if their opinions match your own values.

That might sound like strange advice from a leadership coach – you might expect me to focus on how others perceive your communications and leadership – but it comes from my own experience.

by Sarah Morgan

One discovery I've made over my career is that many women have an identity crisis when they try to combine marriage, motherhood and careers. I am not alone when I say we feel like there is a mismatch between who we are trying to be and what we think people expect from us. It can seem like there are two separate people living inside our bodies: one wants to help others, impress and satisfy; the other feels like running as fast as she can because those voices will never stop telling her different things. Until one day, everything gets too loud for both. Sometimes, a significant event makes us STOP and take stock of where we are and ask ourselves, "How did I get here?"

For me, the significant event was losing someone close to me. This led me to feeling unproductive at work due to both the shock and the depression that followed. I had brain fog, it felt like I was coasting, weighed down, overwhelmed and this was causing lacklustre productivity. Eventually, I was only doing tasks out of habit. My passion had disappeared. In short, I wasn't myself and didn't recognise the person I'd become.

This was when I first went through the process of understanding what is most important to me, through eliciting my own values. I was disheartened to discover a shadow value emerged. A shadow value is one you are operating by even though it doesn't serve you or how you want to see yourself. For me, the shadow value was valuing significance and being important to others.

The problem with this shadow value was that it became a driving force leading me to say 'Yes' far too often. I wanted nothing more than time with family or friends, but I kept saying yes to things which took that time away!

Once I understood what my driving values really were, I could let them lead me in life's journey.

My values of family and helping others were at the forefront as soon as they became apparent. So, there I was... conflicted. I was saying 'Yes' so that I could help others, but that took away from family time. How could I operate when my values opposed each other?

Then it hit me. I was still working for someone else where my life's purpose wasn't being met. I knew making a change was required. Even though there were some significant financial benefits to that role, none of them added up to anything that was getting me closer to reaching my personal goals. I wanted to build equity within myself. Eventually, it became clear... my self-development was my most important and significant journey at that point. I needed to put myself into a mindset of believing in everything I was good at. Also, it meant taking action towards achieving success through any means necessary.

I decided to fulfil my value of helping others through my work, so I would still have time for family. I left my secure job and retrained as a coach. Over time, I developed the Influential Leader Program based on my own and others' experiences in finding their way in business and the corporate world.

One of the most significant changes was to put my priority values first. Nowadays, I say “No” when they are compromised. Saying ‘Yes’ still happens, but I set parameters around what that looks like with time, future potential and giving back.

Going through this journey meant I had finally transformed into a person who was capable of making positive changes in her life. Initially, it didn’t seem like much. But soon I became more comfortable with me. Confident.

And guess what! Things started going well for a change.

Why?

Instead of always being frustrated or disappointed, I taught myself the art of contentment. You see, previously, if I was chatting with a friend about all sorts of screwed-up feelings related to previous events, I’d start to feel negative. Now though, I give myself permission to sit happily with disappointment and frustration. Such liberation!

I'm sure some people will say, "But hang on to those old memories and feelings." Well, that isn't advice I would take unless I was trying desperately hard to be unhappy.

As professionals, we all want to be taken seriously. But in the end, it's easier said than done. You need to be good at your job, you need to show others what you're capable of, and you need to stand out as valuable to an employer. If you don't, nobody will take you seriously or recognise your efforts, regardless of how many degrees or certificates you have. On top of all that, you still need to live happily in your own head. Learning to be content with an imperfect life is a large part of making that happen.

We've all received advice that we wish we had followed sooner. For me, the best advice I ever received was to focus on my own happiness, my own perception of self, rather than trying to please others. To become the leader I wish I'd had. It's easy to get caught up in what other people think of us and to base our self-worth on their opinions. However, this can lead to an unfulfilling life spent chasing someone else's idea of success. Instead, we should concentrate on what makes us happy and fulfilled. This doesn't mean we should ignore the needs of others, but it does mean we should put our own happiness at the top of our priority list. By living a life that is true to ourselves, we can find true satisfaction and contentment.

The other important thing is to learn from your mistakes and keep going. No matter what challenges life throws your way, remember that you have the strength to overcome them. These words may not provide all the answers, but they can remind you of your own inner strength and resilience.

To sum it up, follow your passion and always work hard on what you love and value.

"Sometimes, it's okay to say enough is enough. Every business you start will not be a raging success. That's the cold hard truth."

Lisa Sweeney

Lisa Sweeney

Lisa Sweeney is the CEO of Business in Heels, and for the past 8 years she has focused on supporting businesses and professional women. Lisa loves connecting with women and hearing their stories, "it is so inspirational".

She can't believe she is lucky enough to be able to help them with mentoring, education, marketing & connections.

She is incredibly proud of the work that happens with Mentor Mornings, where experienced women pay forward their support enabling any woman to access mentoring support. "Every little bit makes a difference" and is helping to achieve the Business in Heel's goal to mentor 1.0M women.

Her goal is to enable them to step into their future, to achieve the success they deserve.

Ultimately, her vision is to create an unlimited future for women. Excitingly, 2022 saw the launch of Recalibrate – Gender Equity Awards, which will bring some of that vision to fruition.

She has over 25 years of experience running retail businesses of turnover up to 700M with expertise in strategy, business models, licensing, marketing & digital ecosystems. Today she gets the chance to share this knowledge helping many of the people within her community. She is very proud of the Scholarship programs run to support unemployed women to run a business. It is great to see women go from feeling unsure to confident that they can achieve their dreams.

Lisa loves a great coffee, which is perhaps why her office is above a Geelong Coffee icon, The Coffee Cartel Roasters. She welcomes anyone to join her for a coffee or perhaps a wine if it is late in the day. She lives in the country with her husband, horses, dogs & cats a veritable menagerie nestled in the foothills of the Otway's. In her spare time she loves getting into the bush on her horse or a mountain bike or even out on a surfboard (if the conditions are right).

Website	businessinheels.com
LinkedIn	linkedin.com/in/lisasweeneybusinessinheels
Facebook	facebook.com/businessinheels
Instagram	instagram.com/businessinheelsofficial/

by Lisa Sweeney

The courage to Fail.

I was talking to a mentoring client a while ago. Somehow, we'd strayed onto the topic of parenting, and she told me how her father was very progressive in many senses. In particular, the thing she remembered most was the nature of the dinnertime conversations she and her sisters had with him. She told me he was always interested in our failures. Routinely, he would ask... "How many times did you fail today?"

Initially, she told me, we three children would look at each other and try not to attract his ire with our stories of all the things that didn't go to plan. Eventually though, one of us would tell a story of a failure at maths, geography or in the playground. For some reason, we thought that would result in his disappointment, something no child wants to be on the receiving end of from a parent. But not our dad. His genuine admiration for our failures was stunning.

When friends would come over for dinner, she continued, and the usual topic was on the agenda, they'd be staggered by his response to our failures. "Excellent! Wonderful! Good on you!" he'd say with one hundred percent sincerity.

After dinner and in our rooms, our friends would ask gingerly... "Um, yer dad. Aah, is he all right?"

What they didn't know was the same thing my client learned early whilst growing up, and frankly, I wish I'd learned sooner than I did.

Success comes from failure.

It comes from trying and failing and trying and failing and trying again until you don't fail. Edison didn't invent the light bulb on the first attempt. The Wright Brothers didn't soar up to the clouds the first time. And, chances are, your first few attempts at unlocking the code to your business won't be plain sailing either. Yes, chances are, you will suffer the indignity of several failures before you hit your stride and this will help you assess your appetite for risk.

A business partner and I had a wonderful idea a few years ago. We were going to put together a range of fully customisable leather goods for travellers. This would allow customers to pick exactly what they wanted thereby fixing an ongoing frustration of ours. With our combined buying and ranging skills, which we developed over many years at Target together, we thought this would be something we could do without too much risk as we knew manufacturing processes, had contacts, were confident the goods were saleable, and they were to be supplied on demand out of India which significantly reduced the risk to us.

Yep, it all sounded like a gravy train.

Then reality hit. The nature of the business was that customers were required to custom build, via the internet, the goods they wanted. We had choices for tags, tassels, embossing, colours and more. In fact, we had so many options customers were overwhelmed and we had a huge number of abandoned carts on our site.

Okay, let's fix that.

We did. The next problem was the wait time between the placement of the online order and the delivery of the product to the customer. Okay, we needed to streamline our processes and cut out the delays. We did, down to five weeks out of India... and really five weeks is not that long. What was wrong with those customers!

But still the delay time was too long and customers were not prepared to wait. Consequently, we simply weren't getting the sales we'd forecast. So, we completely changed course and invested in wholesale to produce ranges for stores.

Just when we thought we had everything nailed down, a man in China ate a bat and the travel industry went belly up overnight.

Yep, we were just another business to suffer due to COVID.

Or so we thought...

One of the effects of COVID was for the federal government to begin underwriting various commercial grants. One of these was for R&D. (We had invested heavily in software R&D to get our business off the ground. You see, we needed to create a whole new software program which enabled customers to photographically build their leather goods online with the various options we offered. There was a lot of trial and error. Very nervously, we'd sent tens of thousands of dollars over to Hungary, yes... Hungary, to a software outfit that was capable of engineering this!)

Anyway, we applied for and received a grant and got the flock outta Dodge to cut our losses as there was no end in sight for COVID at that point. With hindsight, this may or may not have been a great decision, but, well... hindsight is only useful after the fact.

The point is this; there is rarely a straight line to success in business. Even with years of experience in the buying field between us, we both did not foresee all the issues that arose. And while we could have put it on ice and restarted at some time in the future, my partner and I both looked at each other and we knew the other had had enough. We both had other irons in the fire we wanted to concentrate on.

Sometimes, it's okay to say enough is enough. Every business you start will not be a raging success. That's the cold hard truth. Just make sure you give it a red hot go before you throw in the towel. Have a plan B, C, D, E and F. They may never be enacted, but they're there just in case and that may provide some comfort. It's also a good idea for the final of your plans to be an exit strategy if it all goes pear-shaped.

I think back now to the conversation I was having with my client about her father's reaction to failure. He was a sensible fellow. He was conditioning his children to try and keep trying. He wasn't conditioning them that success is the only acceptable outcome. It's not. A business is one facet of your being. Don't tie your whole life to its outcome.

“I’m fine!

For those who don’t know, when you hear FINE – think Freaked Out, Insecure, Neurotic and Emotional!!!”

Kistin Gunnis

Kistin Gunnis

Kistin Gunnis has worked internationally and domestically in the Telco Industry and knows how hard it can be to succeed as a woman and on your own merit.

Kistin is passionate about supporting women to win the rewards they deserve. With over 25 years of experience in Operations Management, she has seen it all.

Today, she works with businesswomen to understand and articulate their value and how to make a difference in their profitability. Firmly believing that by educating others about the unspoken rules in organisations and helping people to understand themselves and give themselves permission to achieve and ask for what they want, will expand diversity and increase engaged individuals in the workplace. Kistin is also a leader with Business in Heels.

In her personal life, Kistin recently moved to the Barossa Valley in SA with her husband and has taken up dehydrating and preserving the amazing local produce, whilst also searching for hard-to-find cookie cutters (now at 300 strong) for those all-important cookie-making days. Kistin loves travelling and learning new cultures and is planning to split her time between Australia and Italy upon retirement.

LinkedIn | linkedin.com/in/kistingunnis

by Kistin Gunnis

From No to Yes!

Mentoring others, based on my own life and career experiences is something I do with passion. Over the last few years, my focus has been on providing others with a different view on how they can create the career journey that makes the most sense for them and their family.

I regularly share with my mentees one of the biggest highlights of my career which allowed me to create a role that I loved and facilitated the opportunity to travel globally and grow into the person I am now.

Allow me to share with you this story and my biggest piece of advice – From No to Yes!

I was in a role where I had spent 12 months travelling between Sydney and Melbourne every week, which led to me being not just tired, but flat-out exhausted. I had become the Queen of saying No to everyone and when people asked me how I was, I responded with, by Kistin Gunnis

I'm fine! For those who don't know, when you hear FINE – think Freaked Out, Insecure, Neurotic and Emotional!!!

Due to increasing levels of conflict between distinct groups within the organisation, my stress levels were through the roof, and I had come to the realisation that I had overstayed my welcome in the role. Additionally, it wasn't the best role for my talents, skills, and experience or where I could make the most impact.

I had arrived at a point where people approaching me put me on edge, the phone ringing had me wanting to throw it as far as I could, and I dreaded the next problem that was put in front of me.

In fact, I was done – put a fork in me done!

During a particularly difficult week in Sydney, where I couldn't go to the toilet without people wanting to follow me, I came to the realisation that I could not keep doing what I was doing. Something had to change, and it needed to be me.

I started to look beyond what was on my own plate and realised that for our Business Unit to meet our annual targets we needed an Operations Manager in the APAC region. Otherwise, this was going to become a strategic risk in our region. After a couple of conversations with the Operations Managers in the Americas and EMEA, I had the biggest epiphany.

It was as though the job description for the Operations Manager role was a checklist that reconciled with all the roles that I had had so far. It was a checklist that I could mark off against my resume.

On the flight back to Melbourne, I could feel the excitement creeping back in. I hadn't felt this way in such a long time. It came as a bit of a surprise!

I started a checklist of my own, with the heading, how do I become the APAC Operations Manager?

Firstly, I had to ask myself – What did the executive team need and want?

Once I was able to answer these questions, then I drafted a Business Case answering each of these questions. The language and format of a business case was something the Executive team understood and was in a framework which showed that I was solving a business problem and closing the gap on an understood risk.

Things moved quickly for me from there on. I presented the Business Case and within a few weeks received the authorisation to create the role in the region. I had also budgeted for my own replacements and secured an additional team member for my new team.

By communicating in a language, the Executive Team understood, I created my own role where my needs and the organisation's need dovetailed well, and I could finally do things that better suited my skill set.

And to top off the story, within another 18 months, I became the Global Operations Manager with a team of nine amazing people in seven countries. I supported our Executive

Team through the provision of advice and was sought out on high-profile cross-company projects. I travelled internationally and domestically and had the opportunity to meet and work with diverse and talented people on exciting projects.

For me personally, it allowed me to cement my foundational view of the value, experience, and skills I brought to the table.

When mentees and others hear this approach, it resonates with them, and they often see a clearer way forward. Then we're able to work together on how to make their career dreams come true.

Believing in myself was important. So too was giving myself permission to reach for something different. However, I think the most crucial element was that I met my needs by meeting the needs of others and documenting it in such a way that a Yes was a given.

There was no downside to writing the business case. If the APAC executive team's response was No, all I had lost was the time it took to write the document. I still had a role that was challenging daily.

The moral of my story... whilst I was still the Queen of No in my Global role, I had learned the important lesson of how to move No to Yes!

"It was as though the job description for the Operations Manager role was a checklist that reconciled with all the roles that I had had so far. It was a checklist that I could mark off against my resume.

...

By communicating in a language, the Executive Team understood, I created my own role where my needs and the organisation's need dovetailed well, and I could finally do things that better suited my skill set."

Kistin Gunnis

“The fatigue, boredom and anxiety that so often accompanies the presence of a newborn was debilitating me inside and out. I needed a circuit breaker. I needed a mental distraction.”

Karen Tisdell

Karen Tisdell

An early adopter of LinkedIn, Karen Tisdell recognised the platform's potential when working as a recruiter. Foreseeing the importance of how business leaders are perceived online, Karen began her LinkedIn profile writing business in 2009.

A decade on she ranked as one of the top 8 independent LinkedIn trainers across Asia Pacific and was awarded in 2022 by LinkedIn as a 'Top Voice' for having produced some of the most popular and helpful content.

A listener who dives deep into people's stories to uncover what matters most to them, Karen is passionate about helping women stand out in a way that feels authentic. She articulates their unique value propositions, empowering them to show up on LinkedIn with intentionality to attract the right people and cut through the noise.

Karen is a guest writer for various publications including Inside Small Business, she teaches LinkedIn to MBAs at Sydney's UTS Business School and facilitates LinkedIn sales training for some of the biggest companies in Australia – all while writing profiles for individuals who want to be seen as the go-to expert in their field.

Website	karentisdell.com
LinkedIn	linkedin.com/in/karentisdell
Facebook	facebook.com/KarenTisdellLinkedIn
Twitter	twitter.com/karen_tisdell

by Karen Tisdell

Stand Out and Reject Expert-Ease

Everything about me is average, and for most of my life, I saw this as an advantage, something I could hide behind.

As a child, I wasn't particularly loud. My mum, who came from a different era, encouraged me to play nice. Don't be disagreeable. Don't have too many opinions. Don't take up too much space and do what it takes to be friends with everyone. My dad instructed me to converse about safe topics only. There was no place in polite conversation for my ideas about religion or sex or politics.

Looking back, my timidity was more nurture than nature. I was skilled at being all things to all people. I was a perfectly average chameleon prepared to flatter and appease. But then, I started my own business.

After 14 years in recruitment (which was really a sales job), a wedding, and shortly after, a newborn, I was wrestling with the idea of returning to work. I mean really wrestling!

The fatigue, boredom and anxiety that so often accompanies the presence of a newborn was debilitating me inside and out. I needed a circuit breaker. I needed a mental distraction. I needed to be more than a life delivery system who also put dinner on the table when her man come home from his day at the office. I needed a job. I also needed to be a mother.

So, I created the perfect compromise and started a business at home.

It was the early days of social media, but I recognised the huge potential of LinkedIn as a tool for professional networking and personal branding. I became an expert, and my clients hired me to write compelling profiles that increased their visibility and attracted clients of their own. I faced a couple of personal setbacks (a wobbly marriage and two miscarriages, one at 11 weeks and one at five and a half months), but something clicked, and I had a regular stream of clients coming my way.

One of these early clients gave me the advice I needed to hear all my life: I don't have to apologise for my opinions.

I was writing his resume (which I don't do anymore) and LinkedIn profile. His wife was a writer, so I wondered why he didn't ask her to do it. Why me? The answer was illuminating. He wasn't only paying for my skill. He was paying for my expertise. He needed his LinkedIn profile to attract opportunities, and while his wife could surely compose something appropriate and grammatically correct, she couldn't give him the competitive edge he so badly wanted. But I could. He wanted my advice, and I should back my ability to give it.

It's so hard to see the sea you swim in. It's almost impossible to be objective about yourself and what you offer. But his pushback was a lightbulb moment. We, as experts, become even more valuable when we refuse to give our clients what they think they need. Our service becomes authentic and desirable when we serve our clients' best interests. Only then can we stake our place as an industry authority, a role we have the knowledge, skills, and experience to inhabit, but perhaps not the confidence or self-belief.

I know disagreeing with clients feels counterintuitive. At the end of the day, they pay your bills. Their word can make or break your reputation, and it can feel like their opinion of you is more important than your opinion of yourself. But we must resist, a feat particularly difficult for women conditioned to conform, play small, be quiet, and smile. Or, as Grace Tame put it in an eloquent Tweet, perform "civility for the sake of civility."

Think about it like this: You know something your client doesn't. Even further, you know something that your client doesn't even know they don't know. These unknown unknowns are the crux of your offering, but often, they don't adhere to your clients' expectations. This can make the engagement process difficult to manage, particularly in the early stages.

You need to journey alongside your client. Yes, you can disagree with them. You can uphold beliefs that are polarising and refuse to do what you're told for the sake of it. But you need their buy-in. You need their trust and support. You need to show them evidence and educate them, so they can understand why you insist on doing things a certain way.

A lot of this comes down to measuring the quality of your work on your own terms. A client of mine might be thrilled by the simple addition of correctly placed apostrophes and capital letters. They might see their new profile as sharp and professional, but I see it as bland and forgettable. Unlike my client, I know what good looks like, and a flattering testimonial isn't enough to change my mind. The challenge is speaking up and advocating for what I – for what we, as experts – know is right instead of giving in to what is easy.

Delivering work that you are proud of is everything. Showing up at the table and backing my expertise has helped me gain the respect of others. I have grown from a service provider to a trusted advisor, from just another expert to an authority. Senior executives, in particular, appreciate my candour. They are accustomed to people mirroring their thoughts, so when someone challenges them, they listen intently.

Outside the context of work, my ability to be comfortable in disagreement has helped strengthen my marriage. I can tell my husband what I need. It's a two-way street, and being open to conflict, curious even, means I can shape a life I want.

I know that standing up and speaking up is hard. No one wants to be disliked or thought of as difficult. But trust me when I tell you, it gets easier. Confidence is a muscle; the more you practice, the stronger you become.

It is not about making enemies or undermining others' input. It's about saying, "Here I am. This is what I know to be true. It might not be what you expected or even what you want, but if you trust me, I'll get you where you want to be."

Say it and believe it. Then watch as Little Miss Average turns into a force to be reckoned with.

---

in the series Other books

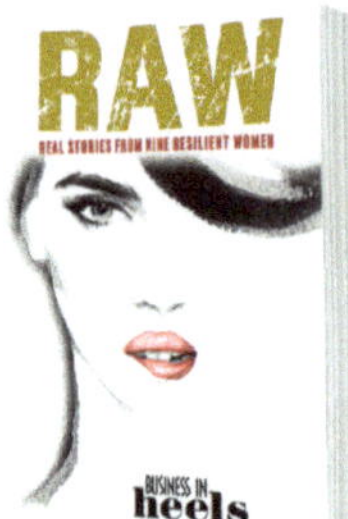

RAW ~ Real Stories from Nine Resilient Women

Shame, Guilt, Ridicule, Poverty, Horror, Impotence, Violence, Fear. Nevertheless, it seems we get an (un) healthy dose of those sometimes too. Mostly, it's not a case of if... it's when. And while you can surround yourself with positive and like-minded people to help you through, when all is said and done, it's those lonely hours between 2am and 4am when we often find ourselves facing our demons.

RAW explores the trials of nine everyday women who chose to carry on. Sure, there's some baggage... but that's a hell of a lot healthier than being continuously beaten up by those demons.

Feeling like it's all about you? It's not. Take comfort from the stories of others who've walked a few miles on some windy, rocky roads through their own barren wastelands...

...and emerged stronger, sharper and ready to get on with it.

Need a new perspective? RAW may help set you on a happier path.

businessinheels.net/raw-book

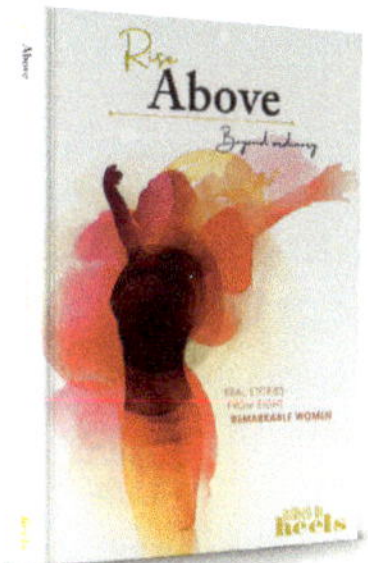

Rise Above ~ beyond ordinary

These are eight remarkable women

Each has a story to tell

Each has a message of hope to share

This collection of stories show the might and power of eight women who refuse to be beaten. Together, they have endured hardship, broken marriages, health crises, catastrophes, self-doubt, parental discouragement, business failure and more.

Yet with grit and determination and fire in their bellies, they have forged on and rebuit their lives,businesses and careers. Their courage, resilience and deep sense of purpose has enabled each to find her path.

Get your copy now

businessinheels.net/riseabove-book-order

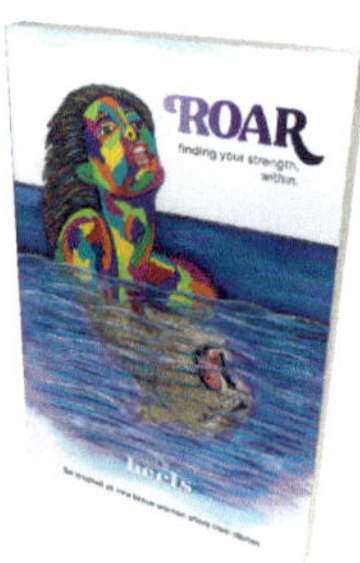

Roar ~ finding your strength, within.

These nine courageous women have gone out of their way to tell it like it is. Prepare to be shocked, to cry, to admire their bravery. Prepare to shake your head in disbelief. Whatever your reaction, know that these women are no longer prepared to cork it, sit still and look pretty.

Prepare to hear them... **ROAR.**

businessinheels.net/roarbook

www.ingramcontent.com/pod-product-compliance
Lightning Source LLC
Chambersburg PA
CBHW040931030426
42334CB00007B/117
* 9 7 8 0 6 4 5 1 6 3 9 3 3 *